Horn knots, Dog pear, And Daisies

A Ranch Perspective on Marriage

By Norma Elliott

About The Author........

Norma currently lives in Alpine, Texas, with her husband Wendel and their two boys, Clay and Jake. They have been married twenty years, serving in youth ministry in various churches, and Wendel is currently serving as pastor at Big Bend Cowboy Church. While writing parts of this book they were living in Carbon, Texas, where they were youth pastors at Leon River Cowboy Church.

Wendel and Norma have faced many challenges; such as, the tragic loss of both of Norma's parents and the loss of their home to wildfire January 2006. Through these difficult times God has constantly reminded them of the parallels of ranching to ministry in marriage and how to hold on to Him and each other through it all.

About the book

Whether you're a rancher or not, everyone can benefit from this book about married life, and how it relates to ranching. Through these simple ranch related reminders, I hope you will laugh and maybe even gain a helpful tip on how to "tie off" to the one you're married to.

The title of this book, Horn knots, Dog pear and Daisies have to do with three things. A horn knot is used to tie off your rope to the saddle horn. I don't know how to rope....yet, but my boys and husband do. I often ask many questions and one of those is about the horn knot-Once you rope a calf, steer, whatever, when your slack runs out it's actually, "tied off" to the saddle horn with the horn knot holding it on. In marriage we must remember-we have "tied the knot" and we are one with our spouse. We are "tied off" to the one we are married to. Thick and thin, plenty or nothing, we are in it together.

Dog pear is that sticky little cactus that jumps on you, your horse, or anything that crosses its path. There are sticky things in life, circumstances couples face that are difficult. Some situations are easily solved while others burr themselves under our skin – just like that cactus.

And Daises......on the cover, there's a pair of leggin's my son, Clay made for me. He could have made me a plain 'ole pair but chose to do a little extra for mom, I guess so I'd be stylin' while workin' cattle. He went the extra mile for me. In marriage, we are tied off to one another by a horn knot, second we come across a few dog pear which try to complicate things, and finally we have daisies- just those extra little things that mean the world to each other!!

With that, I hope you enjoy.........Horn knots, Dog pear, and Daisies

Table of Contents

Chapter 1

Who's the Ranch Manager of this Place?

Whether a place has good or bad ranch management, this is the questioned asked. If the fences are torn down and there's cattle roaming elsewhere; or if fences are mended, cattle are well fed and windmills maintained; either way the reputation of the manager is on the line. Managed well, the ranch foreman is praised for a job well done. Managed poorly, just the opposite, it may be time for a forced career change.

Since being married to Wendel, I have watched his dad manage ranches in West Texas. I have also come to respect and love the five boys he and my mother-in-law have raised, especially the youngest one, Wendel. Growing up their family worked together on ranches, working cattle, loving what they do, and carrying on a heritage.

Ranch Management should be left up to those who know what they're doing. Experienced managers would never leave a doggie calf out in the pasture alone, but he would nurture that new calf by bottle feeding, giving her a dry, warm place to bed down, and watching for any infection or disease.

By now, you are probably wondering what in the world does this have to do with my marriage. Once again I have to ask... Who is your ranch manager? There is only one capable and no the answer is not, "Well, it's my husband; he's the one in charge". Or" It's my wife; she's the one who carries the checkbook." Oh no, this job is beyond human abilities-it takes a bigger than big manager to handle such a task as marriage...His name is God Almighty. The good news, we have access to Him through His son Jesus Christ. These two, along with the Holy Spirit, get the three times All Around Cowboy of the Year.....no wait, Cowboy of the Forever and Ever!!!

If you read back on the description of some of the things a ranch manager does, it's understandable to know that our marriages are in need of that same management, care, maintenance, and plainly put, help by God.

Whether your marriage is like the place described earlier by torn down fences or if it's in pretty good repair, the first and most important thing is to put God first!! Not only put Him first, but to know what He says about marriage and put that into practice.

God as Ranch Manager

Deut. 11:12 "It is a land the Lord your God cares for; the eyes of the Lord your God are continually on it from the beginning of the year to its end."

Matt. 19:5 and said, "For this reason a man will leave his father and mother and be united to his wife, and the two will become one flesh."

Next, we need to talk about the downside. Those downed fences didn't get that way over night; little by little strands may have been weakened by wildlife-traffic, rust, or by being poorly built. Ignoring problems, trying to do it ourselves, or shifting the blame onto others is a sign of poor management or no management. Too many opinions, what others think, what the world might tell us to do, well there's just simply too many managers. I believe the saying is "too many chiefs and not enough Indians." Can you believe it, most of us have tried several of these approaches many times, it's like taking someone from New York City and plopping them right in the middle of some two hundred section ranch (translation: Big Ranch, one section=640 acres)

The size of the ranch alone would be overwhelming for anyone; figuring animal unit per acre, water sources, and varmint control may not even cross his mind. It's obvious to say it would be overwhelming.

I can just picture me, an amateur by far out there telling my father-in-law, Hank which bulls to ship-Ha! That's a joke!!!

I understand that I would not be qualified to do such a job; but because my father-in-law, Hank, has the qualifications as a manager, then he is more than able to carry out the job. I don't know all the answers to marriage...I have been married twenty one years. I'm sure someone who has been married thirty, forty, or even fifty years, has even more to teach me. I hope I have the good sense to listen, watch, and learn.

I trust that God, who created and talks about marriage has seen many, many more marriages-so naturally I want to go to the source, and then put it into practice. Yes, practice.....you can pray, you can read, but unless you practice, well you might as well not waste your time. I believe God is powerful, He can transform some pretty bleak situations but for God's sake don't sit around and expect the cattle to just work themselves-I've never seen a cow vaccinate or brand themselves- so follow what's expected-get to work!!! If the manager, God, show's you something to do then by all means-do it!!

Chapter 2

Cattle Call

Who are you calling out to?

God in the management position has been established-Our ranch is starting to look great, but there's more to it than that, communication!! Yes, how else would the manager get his point across to his ranch hands so they can get to work?

I think of the rancher out in his feed truck. The cows immediately hear the rattlin' of the truck and come running. If the cattle are some distance away, or not within view, sometimes a horn or siren is used to call them up. The siren, horn, or rattling of the truck means dinner time. Notice the call for the cattle comes first, usually a count is taken, cattle are observed, calves are accounted for, and while all are gathered around, feed is delivered. A much welcomed meal in winter and a treat in springtime.

The call....the wait...the feed...God calls....He waits.....we come and He feeds. Matt. 23:37....."How often I have longed to gather your children together, as a hen gathers her chicks under her wings, but you were not willing". *You see the problem is never with God, but with us.*

The rancher goes out, feed truck is full, he honks the horn; the cows have the choice to come or miss the meal. You know sometimes this lone cow will be standing about one hundred yards away or so, she sees the truck, she sees the other cows moving towards it, but still she just stands there chewing her cud, believing what she has is better than what the rancher has to offer. She's probably thinking, "I'm goin' to stay right here and protect my patch of green." Why would she do that?

Once again, let's put God in the ranch manager's position. He calls out to us but sometimes we just don't listen; busyness, distractions, and tons of other stuff tries to wedge itself between us and Him. If He offers the feed; His Word, the Holy Bible; why would we not come and get nourished by it? It's available, in several translations, many easy to understand, just be sure that the translation is a true version. My personal favorite is the NIV: New International Version.

The word is one part of the call. The feed or cake is given to the cows once they are gathered around the truck. The Feed=nourishment! Many scriptures in the Word give us some true marriage advice. I've listed some below that have helped me and are reminders when I am making decisions. I hope they will help.

Proverbs 14:1 "The wise woman builds her house, but with her own hands the foolish one tears hers down."

Ec. 4:9-10 "Two are better than one, because they have a good return for their work. If one falls down, his friend can help him up. But pity the man who falls and has no one to help him up!"

Proverbs 31:10-12 "A wife of noble character who can find? She is worth far more than rubies. **11** Her husband has full confidence in her and lacks nothing of value. **12** She brings him good, not harm, all the days of her life."

Let' talk a minute about the call itself since we have determined the reward for answering the call already. We have determined different resources used to call up cattle, a horn, siren, or the rattling of the truck, but there is another call that is used. This particular call is done with the voice itself; It's kind of hard to describe , with the hand cradled next to the mouth, a sort of howl is let out loud enough for the cattle to hear. This call is repeated over and over until the cows come runnin; the rancher calls and the cows call back, they're saying," I hear ya…..I'm on the way."

Regardless of how the cows are called, this communication takes place between the rancher, cows, and other cattle.

The form of communication I am talking about is called prayer. Prayer is where we pour out our hearts when we are in trouble, to praise our Creator, to ask questions, or receive answers, to ask forgiveness, to stand in the gap for others, and where we listen.

Can you imagine the conversation going something like this?

Rancher....."Do you hear me? Come on in so I can check on you."

Pause......

Cows: "I hear you, I'm coming."
Rancher: "Ah there you are right behind the brush ...now where's the others?"

Cows: "I'm hurrying, I can't wait to eat!! Yum, cake!!"

Rancher: "Good, good, all accounted for.......here's dinner."

Cows: "Yes, we love that rancher man!!!"

Okay I know that may be a silly comparison, but not bad for an example of communication. No we are not cows; girls.......but remember the cow is a beautiful thing in the sight of the rancher.

God's Word, Our Feed!!
God's Call, Our Prayer Life!!!

Failure to Communicate

So what happens when we fail to communicate? We all have communicated poorly with our spouse, we have taken poor advice from people in unsuccessful marriages, and we have run to parents, sisters, brothers, and friends. All these methods are like hollerin' to the guy at the county fair to stop the ride when you know he has no intention of doing so. Talking to our family members or friends is not necessarily a bad thing but when they are struggling themselves or they do not hold what you say in confidence, then, this can cause a wedge between your spouse and his extended family. It's hard for a mom to hear anything negative that her child may be going through and thus making it hard for her to love her son-in-law or daughter-in-law the way it's meant to be. Personally I have shared very little with my family, and I mean very little when Wendel and I have been going through something tough. I have went to very close Christian friends and asked their advice or asked them to pray for us. I believe they do not share my problems with others and do actively pray for us. I do not agree with poor advice, but believe that a wise man (or woman) has wisdom in many counselors........ (Prov. 15:22) and be wise about who your counselors are. First and foremost, communicating with God, then your spouse, and finally wise counsel if needed. I have learned many lessons while sitting in church, Sunday school, or from mentors. Wendel and I try to make it a point to attend some sort of marriage conference or do some type of study together pertaining to our marriage on a regular basis. This keeps us appreciating each other and learning from others who have been there and done that.

How do I find a good mentor? Well, the same way you find a good horse. Check for these three things…..do they have any bad habits? Check out their conformation and finally "watch 'em work"

First of all, do they have any bad habits? When looking for a horse, this is a very important detail you don't want to overlook, not that these habits can't be broken but you'll be further ahead if you don't have to undo a bad habit. One bad habit you can find in horses is called being barn sour, meaning they love….love…love the barn, the comfort it provides and the feed. In fact, they love it so much that they don't want to leave it or when they realize they are heading back to the barn, they take off, running for it. They get spoilt if they are allowed to get away with it.

Next, a horse's confirmation, what do they look like? Okay, be patient with me, I promise this will all tie into choosing a mentor. Anyway conformation on the horse-I can hear my husband's words....he is the horse picker of the family. He would say well proportioned, body-muscled, nice neck and head and all the things one experienced with picking horses looks for.

And finally, "watch 'em work!" This has become a saying in our house, usually after my boys and husband have been out day working. The story goes something like this.....This ole cow was duckin' outta the herd and just lookin' for an opportunity to make a run for it. Next thing we knew, she was outta there. "Ole so and so was nine O in it...) yes the letter O-as in 90-ninety miles an hour!) Anyways ...so and so was 9...0 'in it across the pasture and threw the prettiest loop and tied her to the stump.) Tied her to the stump......tied off to the saddle horn). In other words, "watch 'em work" ....is actually a compliment to the cowboy and his horse.

Alright, here's the fun part-a mentor shouldn't have any bad habits and this can be found out by their conformation-what they are made of. A mentor should be someone who sticks to his principals and faith and you can tell this by "watchin' 'em work"- Now, wasn't that fun?

I mentioned earlier about the order of communication. God first, have you prayed about the situation between you and your spouse? Have you searched His Word for your answer? Have you waited on Him to speak to you? Next, have you communicated with your spouse? Does he even know there's a problem? Does he often hear you complain and has he closed his ears to the next dilemma? Do you start your conversation with blame or asking him questions? How do you handle conflict and how does he handle conflict? All these questions are relevant and timely, and how you approach each problem, conflict, or decision is based largely on your reaction and approach, as well as his. Finally, after taking these first two steps, it would be a good idea for you and your spouse to seek advice.

Chapter Three

Learn the Two-Step

Do you remember when you first learned to two-step? Some of you who are reading may not have two stepped before but you may remember slow dancing at a middle school dance or even a ride along on your daddy's feet when you were little. To me it was kind of like getting on a ride at the fair, my socked feet on top of my dad's huge work boots, I would hang onto his hands and we would glide around the room, effortless for me and great fun. This dance was the beginning of watching and learning. Growing up I observed my parents communicate in good and bad situations. At times their marriage was fun and whimsical; kind of like one of those fast beat two steps, the kind you race out to dance floor for and at other times the dance was a mess, offbeat, and out of step. Their two-step was amazing to me, not because of the mistakes but because of the way it ended. You see my dad had cancer and my mom had Alzheimer's. I saw my parents carry one another just like my dad carried me in my socked feet on top of his big work boots. When my parents were both sick at the same time, my dad would still get up, after chemotherapy and care for my mom's every need, feeding her, washing her clothes, and taking on all the responsibilities. What a beautiful example of a dance. What a beautiful example of a marriage.

When I first danced with my husband, Wendel, I had to adjust to his steps; He being nearly 6'0, and I, 5'4. I had to take long strides so I didn't get stepped on and he had to shorten his steps a little so he didn't trip over me.

The adjustments we make help to make our two step work. At first it may not have been too pretty and my toes got stepped on or he stumbled a little. We tried to quickly recover to get back in step, so that we didn't look like total dance school drop outs on the floor.

In marriage we start off, the excitement of being asked still in our minds, our hearts are racing and our palms are sweating. We laugh about mistakes and take things light hearted, we talk as we dance and get to know one another. Our dance is fun and celebrated, we dance the night away as though no one else is on the dance floor. Does this sound like the beginning of your marriage? You can live in the biggest dump, bills are pilin' up, and you drive a truck that doesn't have air conditioning and drinks about ten gallons of gas every half a mile, but oh it doesn't seem to matter, you've got love. Or, "Honey I forgot to pay the bill" and the electricity got cut off and the reply is "That's okay, we'll eat by candle light tonight, it will be so romantic." The two-step at this point is still fun, its lots of glances, giggles, and goose bumps.

As we progress through our marriage we constantly dance and adjust to steps. We learn to compensate for falls and help each other out so our two-step no longer looks like a middle school dance but now it begins to glide and become beautiful. The longer we dance with one another, the longer we practice helping each other, the two dancing begin to look like one. It's effortless, graceful, and well rehearsed.

My in-laws, Hank and Barbara have been married more than fifty years. I am mesmerized as I watch them glide around the dance floor. They anticipate each others steps and their gestures are almost identical. It's obvious to see the spark in their eye is still there and they truly are enjoying the beat of the western song they are dancing to.

Learn to Dance

Have you ever been to a dance and seen some poor guy out there trying to dance but it just isn't happenin'. He keeps stepping on his partner's feet; he is out of rhythm, and just doesn't look like he wants to be there. Well that's a perfect example of the two-step gone wrong. He wants to sit down and forget the whole thing ever happened. I just love to two-step, I love the sound of the fiddle, and people's feet as they shuffle on the wood floor. I love the sound of the twang of the guitar and the words of a good country song but some people just can't stand it. Now, not all of our friends are dancers and some prefer to just stay home or they would rather take their spouse to a movie or a rodeo, that's fine because the real purpose of learning to dance is just an example I'm using to illustrate working with the spouse to make the most of your marriage.

Some couples really struggle with learning to two step, they struggle with compensating for one another, and helping each other in their dance of life. Some of the ways they fail to compensate for their dance step is through; failing to forgive, pickiness, and selfishness.

Failing to forgive in a two step would be when someone makes a mistake and you just give up and go sit down. Holding on to mistakes in a marriage has the same effect. When we refuse to forgive each other and move on then it's no different than taking a seat. Holding on to one another's short comings leaves a bitter taste in our mouth and builds resentment.

Pickiness in a two step would be like saying, "My partner is just not a good enough dancer!" Pickiness in marriage says, "My spouse is not what I had in mind, she's too loud, doesn't dress the way I like, or is not a people person, like I am." Pickiness in reality is an area of pride, if it's not snuffed out, it sets us up for a fall.

Prov. 16:18 "Pride goes before destruction, a haughty spirit before a fall."

Selfishness in a two step would be like saying, "Adjust to my steps, I am the only one dancing!" Selfishness in marriage is like saying, "Only my opinion counts", "I want it my way!" Selfishness left to itself is just that, it leaves a person lonely because his only thoughts are focused inward instead of outward. God's Word tells us. Phil. 2:3 "Do nothing out of selfish ambition or vain conceit, but in humility consider others better than yourselves."

Chapter Four
Working Cattle

I will never forget the first time I saw my husband, his brothers, and dad work cattle. They all took their place without words, without hesitation, without anything. It's as though they were this well oiled machine, each one doing his part. After saddling their horses, they rode out to the pasture, and after a while they returned, moving a herd of cattle.

As a team, they would ride forward or fall back, working to keep the cows from straying from the herd, so they could push them into one big pen. Inside this pen, some on horseback, others afoot, they separate the cattle. Calves, bulls, and mamas were all separated and each individual group was pushed into separate pens and then into an alley. I watched and hurried for something to do, to be a part of my new family and to take my place. At this particular working I was handed the easy job of secretary, I would mark down number of cows, calves, and bulls to be shipped as they were worked through the chute. I felt proud to be a part and to work beside my family. I felt I had so much to learn and wanted to show respect for those who had been doing it for such a long time.

I noticed the pecking order of my husband and his brothers, the oldest had the rights of either pushing cattle up horseback or taking responsibility of the squeeze chute. The squeeze chute crew needed to get it right the first time so that a cow didn't get away and have to fall to the back of the line to do it all over again. Inside the squeeze chute a cow receives vaccination, wormer, and ear tags if needed. If your hands (cowboys, cowgirls working) are any good, the cattle work runs smoothly and is quite rewarding. The younger hands or buttons usually got the low end of the pole, pushing cows in the alley. Their job requirements include, keeping the alley full and the cows coming. They need to keep on the ball so they don't need to be asked for another cow.

As I worked my little pencil and watched the work around me, I was honored to be part of such a crew. I was engaged in this wonderful work of ranch life.

The best advice I received on my wedding day was a surprise to me, but time and time again I have remembered these words, "Now the work begins." I thought this so strange at the time because I thought the work was over, I caught the man, we were married, what's done is done! How funny my face must have looked when I was given such advice.......I thought she had lost her marbles. Ha...Ha....was I about to understand loud and clear. "Now the work begins." After our honeymoon stage in marriage, I found I was still so much in love with my tall, handsome, Wendel but I had lots of work to do in order to be a good wife.

One of my first task as a wife was to learn how to cook. I was an agricultural major in school and I never found much interest in cooking. The expense of eating out was beyond our budget and in order for us to make it on our income (Wendel was working on a cutting horse ranch at the time) I knew it was up to me to do well on the grocery end of the deal. I burnt several biscuits, made some pasty gravy, and fried everything until it was a crispy critter. My cooking took lots of work before it was recognizable or edible. My cooking was an act of love for my Wendel which required work.

I had to work on my attitude and keep it in line. When you are young and in college you take advantage of simple conversation and allow anything to come out of your mouth. I had to learn to watch my words. I learned that I needed to treat Wendel with respect and that he was also my friend. It's funny how we think its okay to treat our spouse badly but would never talk poorly to a friend. I watched out for things such as, speaking poorly of him in public, negative joking, or rude or embarrassing comments. Speaking well of your spouse gives him a boost whether he is present or not. Everyone enjoys being bragged on a little!!

Finally, I had to work on being a good learner. I had to come to the realization that I didn't know it all, but if I would become a better listener and pay attention to those who had paved the road before me, that I could gain valuable wisdom. I had to learn ways to love my spouse even more. I know that Wendel would agree with me about the work end of marriage because he too was in the process of working on being a better husband to me. We must always remember the work end of the deal or we become lazy and slack in our marriage.

Be a Diligent Worker or a Good Hand

There's nothing more embarrassing to me, than to be in the same room as an arguing couple. There are some things that are better left to private quarters and this would be one of them. All of us have disagreements but to decide that the block party is the time to hash it out, well, bad idea. I have seen friends of mine who have either been the receiver of an inappropriate comment, from his or her spouse, or they have been the one to dish one out. The person receiving the lovely, harsh words is totally humiliated and will loose confidence in their spouse's ability to play nice. Some couples think it is so funny to tease each other with humiliating comments but in reality it is embarrassing and is to no advantage to those who are looking for years of success.

If someone is a slacker at cattle work and they are a day worker (they make their living working cows by the day), then the word around the area would not be in his favor. When choosing day workers you want a hard worker who will help you get the job done. A good day worker usually keeps very busy because ranchers are interested in him. A slacker has a bad reputation and the word gets out quickly not to hire him.

You've been at Cow Camp too Long

Someone who is slack in their marriage doesn't want to learn, listen, or advance. A slacker in marriage becomes too comfortable in his or her own abilities instead of taking opportunities to romance one another. I want to be the best lookin' woman my husband sees all day when he comes home. Keeping up my appearance, taking good care of myself, and having a good attitude are all important. He does the same for me, he has never asked me to lose weight, wear my hair a certain way, or discourage me in anyway about my appearance. I appreciate him for who he is and don't ask him to change anything. Out of respect for each other we have both found it important to look good for ourselves and each other. I still love the smell of his cologne when we are slow dancing and love his starched jeans and shirts. He loves when I wear a sexy little dress with heels when we go somewhere special.

Being a slacker in the area of appearance might be hanging out in your pajama bottoms all day. Never getting a hair cut, bathing only on Sundays, or growing mold on your teeth, these things may be a sign that you've been at cow camp just a little to long. Your appearance should say, "Come home from cow camp honey, mamas waiting."

Chapter 5

Cookie!! What a Feast!!

The ranch cook is a huge asset to the ranch. Cowboys will brag about what they ate during cattle work at so and so place for weeks if they had a good meal. Cookie is sometimes the name given to the ranch cook. The meal is usually incredible with all the fixin's: steak, potatoes, beans, homemade rolls that melt in your mouth, and sweet tea. Banana pudding, cobbler, and chocolate cake are all good ranch desserts. A good cook could be the reason a day worker chooses to come work at one ranch for a little lower wage than a ranch with higher wages serving sandwiches, and gritty tea. At the foreman's table the food is good, the conversation is good, and there are plenty of both.

The best cook I know is my mother-in-law Barbara. She makes the most delicious rolls that you have ever tasted, they are incredibly good, I'm talking about major fights breaking out to get to the last one. The daughter-in-laws often argue about who has the exact recipe for the rolls……..I personally think Grammy (Barbara), likes to see us joke about the whole thing. One time I decided I was going to hide behind a wall and poke my head around every now and then to see what she was putting in the rolls. I found no new information but thought the secret was in leaving the wooden spoon in the bowl while they rise. I went home and tried this method but didn't get the results I wanted. Next, I thought it might be in the bowl she used, so once again I used the same kind of bowl and still got something that looked like a ran-over biscuit. Finally I just asked and watched and practiced, practiced, practiced and my rolls came close but not exactly as wonderful as hers. What a simple and wonderful delight to eat a homemade roll.

I could go on and on about ranch cooking. I could talk for hours about how much food is on the table and how I usually eat so much that I have to unbutton my jeans to find relief. There is nothing in the world like working hard in the pens and then sitting down to a meal that is home cooked. A preparation for such a feast takes hours and may even start the night before. The work is hard and is definitely an act of love. I found my place during cattle work was no longer as secretary, but I had to find out more about those rolls.

Good conversation is another ingredient needed during dinner time. The meal is out, consuming most of the table, but the icing on the cake is the conversation during the meal. Gramps (Hank), is tops among story tellers. His stories usually consist of past cattle work, family history, and funny bloopers. Nobody leaves the table without laughing, not because they have to but because the stories are so great. Laughing together and remembering family history binds our family together and gives the younger family members a sense of their past.

There is a feast in marriage, being together, creating memories. Remembering good times and holding on in bad times. We have a good friend right beside us, the Word tells us that He who finds a wife, finds favor from the Lord (Prov. 18:22). If a wife or husband is God's favor then don't you think it's something to be enjoyed? I wonder how long some of us go before we stop and enjoy the feast at the table. How long do we go between good conversations with our spouse? Are we always focused on the bills, the kids, or our problems? Have we forgotten the art of preparing a meal for one another?

There's no doubt that in our fast paced, want it now society, we often forget to slow down enough to get to know each other. We forget to dream, recall fond memories from the past, and pass on traditions for the future. Just like the feast that was put on the ranch table took time, it wasn't picked up at the drive thru and we can't build marriages at the drive thru of life. Setting problems aside from time to time to recall why the two of you fell in love in the first place is a good starting point.

Another feast in marriage is our love life. Song of Songs is full of the delightful relationship between a man and a woman. It's so unfortunate that media often takes this divine gift and totally distorts it. Sex outside of marriage in any form is not from God; it is sin and displeases the Lord. Young couples often struggle to find that they feel it is dirty or wrong and struggle to enjoy the spouse they have been given. Realizing that sex was indeed a gift that He gives to married couples is one of the most freeing messages married folks need to hear today.

Enjoying one another in the area of conversation, time together, preparing and remembering, and in our love lives, these things are indeed a gift from God.

There's Nothin' like Home Cookin'

I wonder how it happens......you know that sad couple sitting across from each other in a restaurant, a blank look on each of their faces. Nobody says a word at their table, but they are there for, only one reason.......to eat. Yes, that is indeed what a restaurant is for but it seems so sad that the couple doesn't engage in conversation. Not all dates with our spouse are some fairy tale; some dates don't go so good. I remember being on a date with Wendel one time when the waitress was obviously flirting with him, I was mad! Didn't she see me sitting right across from him...."Hello! I have the wedding ring on my hand and so does he!!!" Still this didn't seem to bother her one bit, she kept coming back over to our table and offering my husband tea and didn't notice my empty glass. Wendel wouldn't even look up at her, he was embarrassed. Finally, he asked her to fill my glass and we tried to enjoy the rest of the evening by leaving the table and hitting the dance floor. Not one of our best dates, but we laugh about it now.

Oh, I can hear it now.....date?   What date? I haven't had a date with my spouse since before we married. If you haven't dated in awhile don't feel so bad, but don't feel good enough to continue in your ways, time to get started. It doesn't take a whole lot of money or a whole lot of time. This is another way we can take an example from the ranch life. A long time ago couples used to take a picnic and head off toward the pasture or tank. They would take a walk, go for a ride, or even drink a glass of ice tea under a tree. The purpose of the date is to keep on getting to know each other. Taking your time preparing a date is so much fun. Your spouse would probably smile ear to ear if he or she knew you put a little effort into the time you spend together. Recording the songs the two of you listened to while you were dating is a sure way to his or her heart!!

Settlin' for Gritty Tea and Sandwiches!!!

Do you remember the couple I mentioned earlier? They were sitting at the restaurant with nothing to say, there was no excitement in their eyes, they just existed together. If that has already happened start working on finding out more about what interests your spouse, apologize for anything that might have hindered conversations in the past, and start.....at least start, it's better than giving up. If you or your spouse has given up, all is not lost, pray, pray, and wait. God is amazing about taking our desperate situations and turning them around. Be willing to listen to what God has to say once you pray. He may ask you to change or He may ask you to continue to pray for your spouse's heart to be softened.

Experiencing a feast in our marriage is what God intended for it to be. Don't settle for anything less, be willing to take the time to prepare the meal, by that I mean, be willing to take the time to invest in your spouse. Take the time to find out their interests, have conversations that can be plain and simple and not always having to be related to a problem, plan dates, and be present in their life.

Chapter 6

Rain or Drought

Lately we have been cuttin' lots of coastal hay. There is so much hay in our area that the ranchers are beside themselves trying to get it all baled before the next rain. Here it is the middle of June and we are still receiving a fair amount of rain. Texas usually has some spring rains and fall rains, in between it is usually hot and dry. Why is this a good thing? Well, when we have rain, we not only have feed for cattle, horses, goats, and sheep, but we also have income from hay crops. We all like income, right? This time of year is a good time. Nearly everyone has a smile on their face because things are going well and the cattle are fat. Fat cattle are every ranchers dream!

Let's face it; every married couple can look back on good years of their marriage. I can think of several good years right now and I can think of a few bad years, but we will discuss that in a little bit. The good years might include the birth of your children, a marker anniversary, a job that the two of you enjoyed doing together. Years where everyone was healthy and everyone seemed happy. These years are the years the rains came down and you seemed to be showered with blessings from Heaven.

I remember when our boys were born. We were living in Abilene at the time, still very young in our marriage; we had just bought our first little place and were working on fixin' it up. I look back and smile at the memories. They really do pass by too quickly. Our oldest son, Clay, would have me record him putting on a country music concert ….he was only three at the time. Our youngest, Jake would clap and cheer him on. I also think back to them riding their first horse, Navy. They loved riding with Wendel and by themselves……this made them feel just as big as dad. These years were sweet and the pictures I have of the boys during this time triggers some of the best memories. Now the boys are both in high school and I can think back to many good times since then where our marriage and family just thrived. I can think back to when our income was enough and that which it didn't cover was provided one way or another.

On the ranch, when it rains one of my favorite things to do is check rain gages. We load up in the pickup and ride all over the ranch checking gages that are usually, on the fence posts. Of course, the amounts differed from pasture to pasture and at first, I wondered why it was so important to check them. I honestly thought it was just a way of passing the time since the mall was so far away……ha-ha! Anyway, the reason for checking the gages was to know where to move cattle next, as to where the grass would be growing. The cattle were not moved each time it rained but when their grazing was complete in one pasture then they could be moved to the next depending on which one looked the best.

If you are in a time of plenty in your marriage, the bills are paid, everyone is healthy, happy, and basically things are good...... congratulations!! Enjoy it and don't feel guilty. Some people have a hard time just enjoying life, but here you go, you have permission to have fun. Its okay, you will begin to relax after you see how easy it really is to let loose.

Go Ahead, Check Those Rain Gages and Enjoy the Rain

Drought can be a profit buster to a ranch, due to lack of pasture for cattle. Feed bills rise and if the drought doesn't break soon then it can mean the rancher may have to sell the cattle for low prices. No rain equals no grass which equals no pasture for cattle to graze. No pasture to graze means no profit for the ranch. Not a good time to buy unless you live in a part of the country that receives rain, then you ship those hungry cows up your direction and turn 'em loose.

Last year our community like many others experienced drought. Brown grass crunched under foot and burn bans were a common occurrence. Day after day we experienced clear skies with no chance for rain. Everyone prayed and prayed and prayed, but the rain just didn't come. Wildfires began to pop up in local communities, devastating stories began to surface. It sounded like something out of a horror movie, but unfortunately it wasn't. On January 1, 2006 we lost our home to a devastating wildfire. We were able to get our horses, sheep, and dogs out before evacuating. The high winds blew and smoke blanketed the sky as we drove to a safe location. We waited along with friends from church, anticipating the fires path. Late that evening we learned our home, one of many homes, was completely destroyed. All our memories, families' belongings, and dreams seemed to be gone in an instant. Our family huddled together, in the yard at a friend's ranch. We bellowed a loud, sobbing cry in disbelief that this could be happening to us. That was enough, we were tired, emotionally wrung out, and all we wanted to-do was go home and go to bed-but there was no bed to go home to.

I have had the most difficult time writing this chapter, which has surprised me. I thought when I began this book that this chapter would be the easiest since we have recently experienced drought in our own lives. Writing about how we got through this is difficult.......I know it was by God's grace that we made it through, it was tough. I had a hard time just making simple decisions when our home burnt down. I couldn't even decide what to order at a restaurant one night with friends. I don't have all the answers; I don't know what to tell you except what I experienced.

I prayed a whole lot.....and when I was just too depressed to pray or too frustrated to figure it out, then a friend would call, come by, or encourage us in some way or another. It was just enough to get us through that day. I had lots of questions and didn't understand about half of them. It seemed as though any progress we made was at turtle speed and that frustrated us even more.

During this time we also noticed some amazing things that happened such as, an outpouring of everything from items for our home, money, clothing, and even a home that would be moved to our place. Our community came together in full swing, by actively seeing to others needs. Neighboring communities made tons of sandwiches and sent people to distribute them to those working on cleanup. Everything we could possibly think of or mention was usually delivered before days end. What an amazing sight we experienced because of drought. I will always remember this time as one the most challenging but rewarding experiences of my life. God brought our little community together and made us a family.

Don't Burn Out During the Drought

Okay, I hear you......what does droughts have to do with marriage? Well, drought means lack of rain. When you experience lack in your marriage hold on......hold on to God, let Him work. Hold on to your mate; try not to play the blame game, your both in this together. Get rested, exercise, and most of all get into church... a good Bible based church to get spiritually fed.

Looking back on droughts in your marriage can be times that you both can grow by leaps and bounds and new opportunities can surface. Drought is hard, extremely hard and devastating, but only when we fail to see the good that can arise because of it. When we fail to have a thankful heart for all we have and all that God has done then we experience drought in our spiritual lives as well.

Genesis 50:20 NAS: "As for you, you meant evil against me, but God meant it for good..."

Chapter 7
Time for a Swim in the Tank

Imagine a hot summer day, you've worked hard all day and the chores are finally done. You pull off those hot, sweaty boots, and decide to go for a swim in the tank. Swimming in the tank and listening to the windmill turn is one of the most relaxing and refreshing things on the face of the earth.

Most big ranches have water sources spread throughout its pastures. Windmills, common in West Texas, are often used to pump water up from usually hundreds of feet into a tank. The larger tank then has a pipe leading from it to another smaller trough from which livestock waters. Water wells are a source of life for the rancher and livestock.

Time for a swim in the tank means time for some fun, time for refreshment, and time for a break. This chapter is full of ideas to refresh your marriage, your daily life, your home, and your spiritual life. Some of the ideas I have read for myself in various magazine articles and books, and some have been told to me from friends and mentors.

Ideas to Refresh Your Date Life:

- *Break out the games: Cards, Monopoly, Scrabble, or any game that the two of you might like.
- *Get Out: Go out for a date, if the weather is nice bring a picnic and a book of cowboy poetry.
- *Heat it Up: Cook together, put on your makeup, and smell good and get close and personal in the kitchen. Don't make it too complicated or it will turn into a chore!!!
- *Check out your local paper for events in your area: It's fun to check out local artisans or a good western band.
- *Record songs from your dating days and head out to a place where the two of you can dance the night away without interruptions.
- *Take a walk: Keep the conversation light, have fun recalling special memories and reflect on dreams....be careful not to turn it into a to-do list, but set up a time for the two of you to make a list if needed.
- *Try something new: Have you tried skiing, shooting skeet, or fishing? Is there something that you or your spouse have always wanted to try?
- *Saddle up: Go for a horseback ride together.

- *Scavenger Hunt: Yes, this is even fun for adults. I did this for Wendel one time. I knew several business owners so I had him go to each one for a different clue. We ended the scavenger hunt at the zoo. This was great fun…..and out of the ordinary. Don't be an old fogy!!!
- *Draw for the date: Always arguing about where to eat? Try this……write down five different places that you like and have him do the same. Take turns drawing from her bucket and his bucket once a month and that way you both get the food you like. This also works with date ideas…..he may not know that you would like to see a play, play putt-putt golf, or swim in the lake so writing down ideas and drawing could be a nice way to surprise each other with great date ideas. Keep in mind that it is important to respect each others ideas, so don't laugh if he just wants to go watch a baseball game and eat a hotdog at the ballpark….be a good sport, sounds like fun anyways.

Ideas to Refresh Your Home:

- *Clean up: I once heard it said that a person is more likely to get depressed in a dirty house vs. a clean house. Do a little each day to make your home a little nicer, even if it means going through that old stack of magazines and throwing out what you will probably never use anyways. Imagine how good the house will look at the end of the week or end of the month.
- *Keep it fresh: Purchase fresh fruit or fresh flowers and display them around the house.
- *Rearrange: Have you tried the couch against a different wall or better yet moved it away from the wall to take in the best view, such as a big window or fireplace.
- *Try a new recipe: Once a week try something new, you may find a new family favorite. Better yet, try a new super market that carries fresh produce, seafood, or has a killer bakery. Just something that inspires you, that won't break the bank, can revive your cooking routine.
- *Get those photos developed: With today's technology you can send a photo to a super store or photo shop, pick out size and color for very little money. Pictures hung on the walls trigger good memories and tells others the story of your family.

- *Exchange: Have a chore that you just dread? Get a friend to help you in exchange for you helping her with one of her chores. If you dread the chore more than you can bear, hire someone or exchange the chore with a friend for something you like doing better for her. If you like to cook and you have a friend that loves to clean then exchange your talent for hers.

Ways to refresh your daily life:

- *Start the day with praise: It's easy to think of all the things that are wrong in our lives but when we wake up and give God praise first thing in the morning then it gives us a fresh perspective for the whole day. Remember the Israelites wandered around in the desert for forty years because of their lack of having a thankful heart.
- *Learn how to do your job better: Whether you are a school teacher, homemaker, attorney, or business owner, learn how to save time, energy, and money. Pick a mentor, and learn her ways, this will put a spring in your step

and will help you to do your very best for whatever purpose God has currently called you to.

- *Remodel yourself: Don't like the way things look? Try a remodeling job……..such as remodeling a room in your home, your physical appearance, or your education. Keep in mind the consideration of others, don't go crazy with this one, remodeling can mean small changes, but be sure your changes are in line with God's Word and that your spouse agrees with the changes. For example, don't go take out a $10,000 loan to remodel your home if you and your husband have decided to get out of debt.

- *Take a break: Life isn't all about work!! Enjoy your life in work and play, take breaks throughout your day to read, dance, or watch a show that you really love. A walk, a horseback ride, or an art class can be just what you have been looking for to shake things up a bit.

- *Ways to end a day: It's a good idea to end the day just the way you began the day, with praise to God. It's nice to end all your chores such as washing dishes and putting kids to bed early enough to have time to unwind. If you work all the way up until midnight, then you tend to go to bed with a mind that is racing. You will rest better if you decide on a time in the evening to stop working and start relaxing. Try this: wash your face, light a candle, and put on some relaxing music. Even if life has thrown you a curveball this can help eliminate some of the stress.

Ideas to Refresh Your Spiritual Life:

I have saved the best for last…….I hope these last refreshers will boost your spiritual life and that you will be refreshed to follow The Lord Jesus with all your heart, soul, mind, and strength.

- *Be a giver: Give to God your heart, soul, mind, and strength. Matt. 22:37 Jesus replied: "Love the Lord your God with all your heart and with all your soul and with all your mind." The first commandment can totally rearrange your heart and your thought life. What's in our hearts flows over to our thought life, which flows to our mouths and out to our family, friends, and coworkers. Think about what you're thinking about and you will soon see the root of many problems or anxieties.
- *Read the Word: If you have a hard time understanding the Word, then check with your pastor about different concordances, commentaries, or studies. The information available today is vast, so be careful in your selection. Remember the enemy is crafty and

uses trickery to lure you into things that may look Christian but are far from it.

- *Take it to a new level: Have you been doing the same kind of studies for the last five years? Find a study that challenges you and causes growth. Don't be afraid to invest more time into your spiritual life, this area of your life is the most important part of who you are.
- *Buddy up: Try doing a devotional with your spouse or praying together if you are not already doing so. Even if you are not the kind of couple that does devotionals together, just talking about the Lord and coming together, standing on His Word, will cause major changes. The Word says, "Where two or three are gathered in my name, there I am in the mist of them."
- *Go on a retreat: Retreat!!!! I can picture it now; we often hear this word when watching war movies. The army, who is losing the battle, turns and runs, yelling, "Retreat, Retreat!" This isn't a bad idea; we need to keep in mind that we are in a battle......a battle for our marriages, our families, and our beliefs. Retreats allow us the rest and insight that we need to refresh our battle plans. Make your plans to find a marriage conference or marriage retreat today. If your husband just isn't keen on the idea then just plan your own retreat, don't fight with him about it, but just make it a

time to be alone with him and enjoy his company.

- *Journal: Pick up a journal and jot down your prayers and thoughts. Write a love letter to God or imagine what He might say to you. God is crazy about you and His Word affirms His thoughts towards us, Jeremiah 29:11 says, "For I know the plans for you, plans for hope and a future...."

- *Make a book of thanksgiving: Just like a photo album, you can make a book of thanksgiving recalling all the things the Lord has done for you and your spouse. Keep this book out in the open where you can see it and record things on a regular basis. Also, if you feel comfortable, you can leave your thanksgiving book out for others to see. Reading yours and your spouse's story can inspire others.

- *Help someone else: Teaching others the Word or helping younger couples causes growth in your own life. When you are teaching someone else, then you are more likely to research and study. Those older are instructed in the Bible to teach the younger ones. Word to the wise, pray about this one, talk to your pastor, ask to be an assistant to your current married couples teacher and pray to see if it is God's will for you to teach. Don't just go in cold turkey if you are planning on teaching, you want to make sure you are teaching from

God's Word and not just by your own experiences. Teaching doesn't mean you have to do it in a Sunday school setting you can be a teacher to the couple next door or to your coworkers.

- *Do something fun: Spiritually speaking, do something fun, our God is not boring…..so keep in mind that you're spiritual life doesn't have to be boring either. Mix it up a bit and sing a new song unto the Lord.

May the Lord bless you as you bring your marriage to new heights. May He bless you as you follow in obedience to His Word and delight in His ways.

Unless otherwise noted all scripture comes from the Holy Bible, New International Version © 1973, 1978, 1984 by International Bible Society. Published by Zondervan Publishing House, Grand Rapids, MN.